RAFAEL MONEO

RAFAEL MONEO

Marco Casamonti

Motta

Rafael Moneo

Cover
Kursaal, San Sebastián
Photo
Duccio Malagamba, Barcellona

Translation
Clarice Zdanski

minimum
essential architecture library

Series edited by Giovanni Leoni

Published Titles

Mario Botta
Santiago Calatrava
Richard Meier
Pier Luigi Nervi
Jean Nouvel
Renzo Piano
Álvaro Siza

For the excerpts reproduced in the sections
"Thought" and "Critique," the authors and publishers
wish to thank those who have authorised their
publication. The publisher is available for any queries
regarding sections for which it has not been possible
to trace the holder of the rights.

© 2008 Il Sole 24 ORE Business Media srl, Milan
© 2009 24 ORE Motta Cultura srl, Milan
© 2009 Il Sole 24 ORE Business Media srl, Milan

First Italian Edition: May 2008
First English Edition: October 2009

ISBN: 978-88-6413-012-5

Printed in Italy

Sommario

Portfolio

Introduction

Moneo: The Rigour of the Profession

Just a glance through the register of Rafael Moneo's works is enough to make one realize how varied and complex the projects are – whether constructed or not – that the architect has put so much his untiring effort as researcher and scholar in forty years of practising the profession. Today, they number 130 projects, of which 80 have been carried out in different countries all over the world, and we must add dozens of writings and theoretical works, besides his university career, including many years at Harvard.

Nevertheless, once past the quantitative aspect that in any event bears witness to a vitality and extraordinary dedication to architecture, it is important to dwell on the knowledge of the work of the master and the ability and rigour with which the project, understood as artistic and intellectual activity, identifies and deepens the reasons of its own necessity each time. Although within coherent, personal research, each work is the result of a continuous desire to experiment while making clear, drawing after drawing, stone after stone, a refusal to take any sort of shortcut or adopt any merely convenient solution as recourse to a superficial recognizability that at times characterizes the activity of some of the leading figures on the international architectural scene in a calligraphic way.

In his affable, moderate modesty, Moneo defines this disciplinary profundity according to which each project is a new project as a specific "… fear, a difficulty in working with one's own language". Yet there is an absolute continuity in the method and in the logic with which each of his works is resolved, as it is with each of his details, whether technical or inherent in the composition of the building. "I am not – he confessed in the course of one of our recent conversations – interested in knowing in advance what I will do in my next work. I try instead to let myself go when faced with the sheet of paper on the table in front of me. This not being prepared, this being able to take refuge from 'what one must do' is […] the most fascinating characteristic of this profession. This diversity of architecture, that is, the variety that is born of the difference in the situations in which one goes to work, is what I try to celebrate in my work".

The key to reading this analytical interpretation of the conditions that characterize his way of constructing, whether understood as theoretical elaboration or practical activity, is the appropriateness of every solution to the theme, of every project to its own context, of every material with respect to its use and to its technological characteristics. That is why each project reveals a personal yet attentive interpretation of the places and the cities with which Moneo always manages to establish deep, original ties. It is this way with spatiality, allusions to the classical and the use of brick for the Museo de Arte Romano in Mérida, in the sophisticated "Novecento" rationalism spelled out through the stone of the colonnade that designs the vibratile front of the Municipio in Murcia, or the hypermodern juxtaposition of the volumes of the vitreous wrapping of the Kursaal in the bay of San Sebastián. The list could go on and on if, already in these examples, there were not an evident reiterated underlining of a will in which the constructional writing seems to shape itself to variation on the themes, the history and the specific geography of the individual places.

When faced with these different "conditions on the surroundings" Moneo seems to want to listen to his rational as well as pondered instinct that, with constant effectiveness, enables him to identify the aspects that emerge each time as true architectural problems. In each new job, for each new project, for each new place, his way of acting seems to respond to a recurring question: "what do you see?". In so many years of work and with the disciplinary tools that time seems to have refined into an expert disciplinary adroitness, the instinctive manner remains the only true certainty in a way of working that does not know failure, the easing of tension or false passes, all warded off by the intuitive act and the renewal of discovery: "There is always a first moment in the project – Moneo explains – in which you do not know where you want to arrive, you only have your instinct as a guide, and it is one of the most intense moments. But it is just as beautiful, then, to see how things acquire their own clarity by themselves. They gradually become more and more precise, and this is the pleasure of developing the

View from above
Fundacion Pilar
y Joan Miró

project. The greatest satisfaction comes from when, once you've got over the problems, the initial idea comes back to the surface again, the 'answer'. It is important to underline that, during the construction, too, the work puts up a certain degree of resistance to reveal itself as 'complete'. Completeness is something that one reaches only when construction is finished – until then the project 'hides'. The architect is animated by an immense desire to discover how much is closed up in the project – and only in the finished work can it be revealed. It is as if the work strenuously defends this sense of surprise, which construction also reserves for those who have been in this profession for a long time".

Nevertheless, if it is true that every project is always profoundly new and different, in all of Moneo's works, one easily gathers the fruit of the previous work, the essence and the fundamental characteristics of an evolutionary chain of thought that is echoed in a vocabulary rich in spatial, material and constructive neologisms. The cathedral in Los Angeles, for example, and not just because of the polished use of coloured exposed concrete, is in some way indebted to the research carried out for the execution of the Miró foundation, as is Mérida and the exegesis of the application of exposed brick already experimented with for the Bankinter building, while the solution of the repeated juxtaposition of the covering with a truncated pyramid topped by a parallelepiped constitutes the invention of a machine to capture and diffuse the zenithal light that Moneo has used in many of his museums, from Sweden to the United States to the little Don Benito cultural centre in Spain. It is a question of subtle references, of continual moving forward and turning back where each project does not fade into itself, but transmits its innovations and discoveries in later works.

The recent maternity hospital in Madrid shows a singular ability to adapt to a situation and a theme – that especially complex and articulated one of hospital construction – while in the intensive use of glass surfaces there is clearly research on transparency, reflections and translucent opacity at work in the already tried and tested vitreous facings in the San Sebastián Kursaal, even if with a different tactile perception.

Matter and materials assume, as can easily be seen just by observing the sequence of images of his works, an importance and an extraordinary value, a sort of metonymy revealing that a true

"faith" is felt: "In order to explain this concept – Moneo says – I have often referred to the work of my colleagues who speak of abstract architecture. Peter Eisenman for example spoke of architecture that was indifferent to materials and it was thanks to this very indifference that he found its essence in the abstractness of formal structure. I on the other hand have always maintained that the materials are what constitute the substance of architecture, that is to say, that in its material substance, the building has much of what is supposed to be its conceptual essence. Mérida would be another project if the walls were in plaster instead of brick. A building like Bankinter would be inconceivable without that integration of terracotta with the formal structure that ensures that in the piercings of the windows the size of the thickness of the bricks is rendered: this is part of the substance of the building".

In analysing the American projects like the Davis Museum at Wellesley according to this line of interpretation, the accent shifts to the necessity of furnishing a very clear urbanistic answer, initiating accurate work on the meaning and value of a dimension of space that transforms the interior of a building into the substance of architecture. These characteristics probably make the response on materials less incisive and necessary with respect to the European projects, as is demonstrated by the work in Houston. Instead, the case of the cathedral in Los Angeles is different, because, despite an urban condition that organizes and gives meaning to the entire system, the material again becomes protagonist of the architecture by putting itself forward as identical in its massiveness both on the outside as well as the inside of the building. Without this radical choice, perhaps the beauty of the construction would be lost, being resolved instead peremptorily in a unitary act that leads the complexity of the elements back to the whole, from the bell tower to the façade, from the apse to the parvis down to the parochial works that characterize an intervention of exceptional urban size and with an exceptional urban role. From the hospital to the church, from the wine cellar to the museum, from the home to the conference centre, from the office to the theater, from the station to the airport – each of Moneo's constructions brings out its own formal alterity and a decisive will to experiment beyond materials, spaces and contemporary interpretative models.

The latest projects initiate a phase of further

experimentation sustained by the will to investigate the results of non-Cartesian spatiality through the use of concave and convex lines, according to research that works with the idea of the wrapping as an uninterrupted encircling surface.

With the combined use of complex geometries obtained from the composition of fragments of primary figures like the circle and the hexagon, Moneo shapes buildings with articulated, original silhouettes, generating a form that can express his own special inner energy.

In the Beulas Foundation in Huesca, for example, the ability to go beyond the stereometric rigour of consolidated volumes expresses architecture that can establish a silent sequence of plastic relationships with the landscape and surrounding nature. In this way, the spaces generated by the encounter between the base structure and the fluidity of the perimeter acquire a beauty and specific force of their own underlined by the lightness with which the concrete wrapping unfurls in the wind.

In the project for the library in Leuven, in Belgium, the building places the white of the plaster, derived from modern tradition, side by side with the brick, and through the light, plays with the concave and convex surfaces, in such as way as to express a sense of ductility, for architecture that thus assumes its own formal autonomy.

Instead, in the project for the new headquarters of the government of Cantabria in Santander, the architectural solution interprets the theme of a more rigorous stereometric criterion that follows the will to explore the representational measure of a translucent whole. In this case, the building assumes the role of singular element in the urban fabric, equipped with its own specific form, and is for this reason a sophisticated autonomy that is also independent even if well identified and identifiable with respect to the context of the city. Nevertheless, for Moneo the project does not coincide with reaching a certain result; it is not essentially the final phase of a process that can be determined a priori. On the contrary, it is the fruit of a cognisant invention and a conscious admission of the meaning of the arbitrariness of form.

The difference between one project another follows the analysis expressed with respect to the use of materials since it appears to be more accentuated when Moneo works in consolidated urban contexts, more elementary in comparison

with urban realities where the theme of continuity and environmental pre-existences is shown with less evidence, making every decision in the project naturally independent with respect to the context of reference.

Murcia, San Sebastián, Mérida, Pamplona and Madrid highly condition projects that appear as true urban resolutions, while the discontinuity typical of the American reality seems to impose its own specific autonomy on the composition.

The project for the art museum in Houston suggests the idea of exhibit space as a contemporary factory, where the immanence of internal spaces, in a place where the climatic conditions are critical, assumes a central, founding role for the entire building, where life is conceived exclusively as an inner condition.

On the contrary, the project for the city hall in Murcia belongs to the square that it stands on, to the cathedral that it faces, imposing on the prospect a vertical structure articulated by a colonnade in stone. None of the prospects in Houston is designed giving preference to the theme of the façade since no side of the building can be observed frontally, and since there is no direct rapport with the urban space, the system of relation with the surrounding streets is thought out solely in terms of traffic and the use of the automobile, a sort of *machine à habiter* derived from Le Corbusier.

Unlike the theme of the classical, the use of the column and the arch is clearly manifest, not only in Mérida, in the airport of Seville as well. Such references are in any event proposed with balanced insistence in many other projects, while the adhesion to modernity coherently constitutes an element of the unmodifiable in Moneo's work, a work that seems to explore and objectively take over the theme of the classical and the anticlassical. Thus, once again in the construction of the airport, he plays with the comparison between building and airplane, insisting more on their differences than on their similarities. The project thus measures up against an idea of an airport that is iconographically at the antipodes both of today's mechanistic models as well as of a nostalgic historicism, since the classical element is placed in the composition of the whole not in a stylistic manner, but as the sublimation of a function that is not mere channelling of arrivals and departures, but rather a sense of welcoming and participation in the theme of travel.

Seville's is the only airport where one can leave

Opposite page
Interior of the Our Lady
of the Angels, Los Angeles

the car in an orange grove and, when entering, breathe in an atmosphere not far from what envelops the city itself. That is why it does not express a calligraphic classicism, but rather the interpretation of character and a way of living, even if only temporarily, in a place that aims to be recognized as such. The sombre, rational classicism of Murcia does not express the classical in "canonic" form, but rather makes clear a metaphysical dimension that projects onto the building a profound sense of belonging. The idea of a retable, of a fountain, as well as traces of theaters, or better, of the ruins of Roman theaters, was certainly well impressed in the architect's memory, as was the will to enclose in the design of a wall the sense of a becoming that collects in a fragment an entire architectural universe that extends from Vitruvius to Alberti down to Gardella, the architect towards whom Moneo shows a continuous as well as emotional sense of gratitude.

For Moneo, modernity is a dimension that is continually repeated in history, a constant in every architectural period, the desire for change and the search for the new that characterizes every movement and cultural intention:

"Definitely – Rafael Moneo maintains – the characteristic of modernity that most fascinates me is optimism, not at all technology, and this is also because in a certain sense technology is no longer in architects' hands, as it was in the times of Brunelleschi's cupola or of the great Gothic cathedrals". Nevertheless, within the international debate, the architect, who can boast of an extraordinary number of awards and honours besides the Pritzker prize, is in a position of conscious distance with respect to many contemporary architects "and at certain times" confesses Moneo "this is a bit agonizing because I am alone. But at the same time, there is the fact that I can offer to others a different kind of testimonial than the ones that are more frequently listened to. In this sense, without a doubt, my projects are answers and contributions to superimpose on the work of others. That also happens because I still have the curiosity to see what is moving around me. I absolutely do not feel alien to the debate; on the contrary I think it is important that if you believe that there are segments of sensibility open to confrontation and that you feel close to, what you should do is to offer them, even if this does not seem to me to coincide with a very frequent desire".

Chronology

1937	Rafael Moneo was born on 9 May in Tudela (Spain)
1956	During his studies, he worked in Madrid in the studio of Javier Sáenz de Oiza (until 1961)
1961	Took his degree in architecture at the Escuela Técnica Superior de Arquitectura (ETSA) in Madrid Went to Hellebaek in Denmark to the studio of Jørn Utzon (until 1962)
1963	Obtained a fellowship to study at the Spanish Academy in Rome
1965	Returned to Madrid, started professional activity
1965	Diestre Transformer Factory, Zaragoza (finished in 1968)
1966	Started teaching at the ETSA in Madrid (until 1970)
1968	Urumea residential building, San Sebastián (finished in 1972)
1973	Municipio, Logroño, Spain (finished in 1981)
1970	Taught elements of architectural composition at the ETSA in Barcelona Along with others, founded the journal *Arquitectura-Bis*
1976	Taught at the Institute for Architecture and Urban Studies in New York and at the Cooper Union School of Architecture. Taught composition at the ETSA in Madrid
1980	Museo de Arte Romano, Mérida (finished in 1985) Bank of Spain branch, Jaén, Spagna (finished in 1988) Taught at the universities of Princeton and Harvard until 1984, where he was head of the Department of Architecture until 1990
1982	Headquarters of the insurance company Previsión Espanola, Madrid (finished in 1988)
1983	Headquarters of the Collegi d'Arquitectes, Tarragona, Spain (finished in 1992)
1984	Atocha Railway Station, Madrid (finished in 1992)
1985	Held a course at the Ecole Polytechnique in Lausanne
1987	San Pablo Airport Terminal, Seville (finished in 1992) Diagonales Haus L'Illa, Barcelona (finished in 1994) Music Auditorium, Barcelona (finished in 1999)
1988	Davis Art Museum, Wellesley College, Massachusetts (finished in 1993)
1989	Museo de Arte Thyssen-Bornemisza, Madrid, Spain (finished in 1992)
1990	Kursaal Auditorium and Music Centre, San Sebastián (finished in 1999) Don Benito cultural centre, Badajoz, Spain (finished in 1997)
1991	Museums of Modern Art and Architecture, Stockholm (finished in 1997) Fundacion Pilar y Joan Miró, Palma de Mallorca, Spain (finished in 1997) Project for the Palazzo del Cinema, Venice Lido Became Josep Lluís Sert Professor of Architecture at Harvard University Julián Chivite Winery, Navarra, Spain (finished in 2001) Expansion of the Cranbrook Art Academy (finished in 2001)
1992	Received the Municipio di Murcia gold medal of fine arts from the Spanish government and expanded the square in front of it, Murcia, Spain (finished in 1998) Audrey Jones Beck, The Museum of Fine Arts, Houston, Texas, USA (finished in 2000)
1993	Hotel Hyatt in Berlin (finished in 1998)

	Received the Arnold W. Brunner Memorial Prize for architecture, the Principe of Viana Prize on the part of the Government of Navarra, the Schock Prize for Visual Arts

Received the Arnold W. Brunner Memorial Prize for architecture, the Principe of Viana Prize on the part of the Government of Navarra, the Schock Prize for Visual Arts
Plaza de Santa Teresa in Ávila and parking area, Spain

1994   Museum of Sciences, Valencia (finished in 1996)

1995   Royal and General Archives, Navarra, Pamplona, Spain
The Prado Museum Extension, Madrid (finished in 2007)

1996   Received the Pritzker Prize and the gold medal from the International Union of Architects
Our Lady of the Angels Cathedral, Los Angeles (finished in 2002)
New maternity ward and children's hospital Gregorio Marañón, Madrid (finished in 2003)
Beirut Souks, Beirut, The Lebanon
Pollais House, Belmont, Massachussets, USA

1997   Nominated Académico Numerario of Real Academia de Bellas Artes of San Fernando, Madrid
Arenberg Library and Campus, Leuven, Belgium (finished in 2002)

1998   Project for the extension of the Bank of Spain, Madrid
Received the Feltrinelli Prize from the Accademia nazionale dei Lincei

1999   Beulas Foundation, Huesca, Spain (finished in 2003)

2000   Project for the Rhode Island School of Design, Rhode Island, USA
Project for a new physics building for Harvard University, Cambridge
Balneario di Panticosa, Huesca, Spain

2001   Roman Theater of Cartagena Museum, Spain
Homes in Carrer Tres Creus a Sabadell, Barcelona (finished in 2005)
Project for the new headquarters of the government of Cantabria, Santander, Spagna
Received the Manuel de la Dehesa Prize at the VI Biennial of Spanish Architecture

2002   Project for the Spuimarkt homes, Holland
Residence for the Spanish Ambassador in Washington
Project for a bridge and a walkway over the Pisuerga River, Valladolid

2003   Received the Gold Medal of the Royal Institute of British Architects (RIBA)

2006   Received the Gold Medal for Architecture on the part of the Consejo Superior de los Colegios de Arquitectos de España

Works

Presentation texts for the sections "The Works" and "The Projects"
are taken from the project reports drawn up by Rafael Moneo Studio

Museo Nacional de Arte Romano
Mérida, Spain, 1980-1985

View from the entrance

The national museum of Roman art is placed in the modest environment of the city of Mérida, transforming the city itinerary with its presence, and appearing like a sort of anticipation and premonition of the remarkable spectacle created by the splendid ensemble of Roman ruins. The building, which looks out onto the Calle José Ramón Mélida, appears like a series of truncated buttresses that, in the austere structure, make evident one of the principles upon which Roman architecture is founded and that the designer intended to instil in the building: solidity of construction.

Insistence on and repetition of the constructional theme – the buttress – shows, for that matter, the very structure of the museum: the building is both a worthy frame for the already found remains of the past of the Roman city and a repository for future artefacts that will automatically transform it into a living archive. This condition of museum-archive can be noted in the image of the building, seeing the influence that the repetition of the constructional elements has had on it. The will to recall and evoke the Roman past is thus clear: the museum, without imposing the

View emphasizing the repetition of the Roman arch that becomes the perfect "frame" for the archaeological artefacts

severe limits of Roman architecture, wants to suggest to the visitor the order of the dimensions, in the broadest sense that this term had in Mérida's Roman period. That is why Roman building systems were adopted, and it was entrusted to them – and not to the mouldings and orders – to make explicit the proximity to the Roman world, which is the basis for the entire project. Constructing a museum in which archaeological artefacts might find a suitable frame inevitably means alluding to the Roman world and its building system, which gave way to a building whose

wall structure gives the formal support to architecture, where the intervals, proportions, the empty spaces represent essential elements. However, this system is transformed when it meets with interference: the system of voids, which produce the central element of the nave. This was the dominant theme of the project and of the dialectical relationship between the transversal and longitudinal order of the walls created by the void that the arches form from within: thus emerges a space that frames the objects that the archaeologists have brought to light through time.

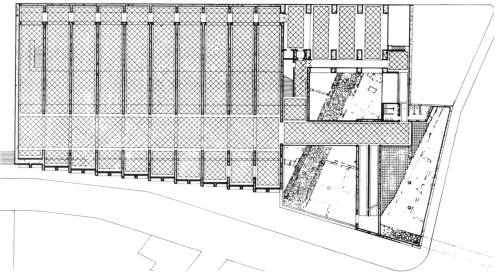

Above and opposite page
System of itineraries
and walkways that
organize the circulation
on the different levels

Left
Ground plan of the site

Kursaal
San Sebastián, Spain, 1990-1999

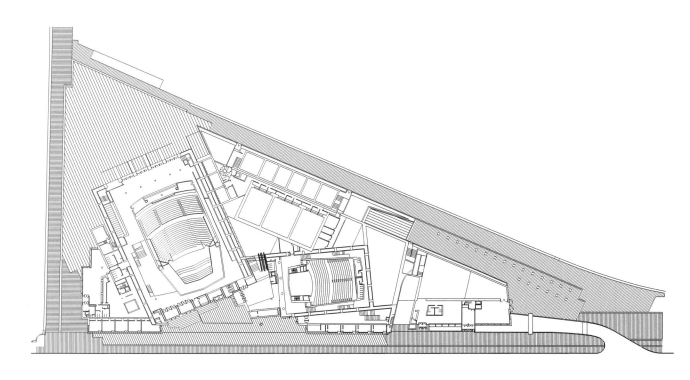

Above
Plan of the ground floor

Opposite page
View of the complex
from above

To say that the beauty of San Sebastián comes from the natural environment and the landscape is little more than a cliché. Few cities enjoy more favourable natural conditions. The Cantabrian Sea calms down on the beach of the Concha and creates, in a brief stretch of coastline, all of the morphologies described in geography manuals: bays, islands, beaches, inlets, mountains. That is why Rafael Moneo's project for the Kursaal is aimed at constructing a building that does not destroy the presence of the Urumea River, since the mouth of the river where San Sebastián was founded is should be visible. The auditorium and conference room are interpreted as two giant rocks run aground at the mouth of the Urumea: they do not belong to the city, but are part of the landscape. The auditorium and the concert hall stand out as autonomous, isolated volumes. The exhibit halls, conference rooms, service rooms and restaurants are contained within a platform that offers an appropriate place for the cubic masses and at the same strengthens their leading role. Moreover, the platform makes it possible to reach a sufficient height to see the sea. It also is open onto the Paseo de la Zurriola, where there is ample space from which to have access to the auditorium, concert halls, conference rooms and exhibit spaces. This zone is connected to the parking area and houses the information point and the ticket office. The auditorium is a prismatic volume made dynamic by a slight inclination towards the sea, "almost a geographic element". The construction ends in a metallic structure that forms a double wall in which pieces of glass are embedded internally and externally, flat on the inner façade and curved on the outer one. The section clearly shows the constructional system, which can create a luminous, neutral interior space in contact with the outside only in the spectacular atrium windows looking out onto the sea. Glass is an appropriate material for San Sebastián, given the position of the Kursaal, exposed to high winds that are at times full of salt water. The glass is the result the of lamination and curvature of a 19-millimetre thick slab and Flutex glass that transforms the volume into a dense, transparent mass that changes colour in the course of the day, and is transformed into an attractive, mysterious source of light at night. Inside the suspended glass prism, inscribed asymmetrically, is the volume of the auditorium. The asymmetry ensures that the space of the atrium unconsciously orients the spectator's steps towards the higher level, from which he or she might contemplate the sea in all of its beauty against the background of Mount Urgull.

Above
Access ramp
for the complex

Left
Sketch

Opposite page
Foyer

Museums of Modern Art and Architecture
Stockholm, Sweden, 1991-1997

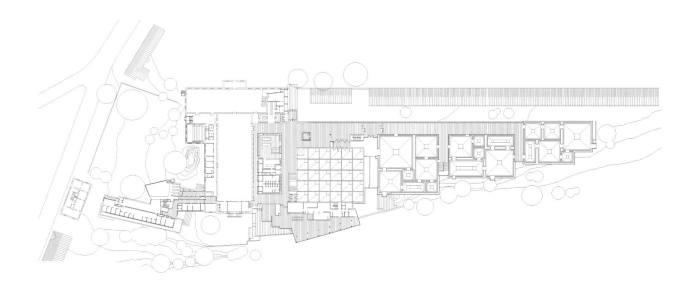

Plan of the ground floor

The Museums of Modern Art and Architecture are located on the island of Skeppsholmen, occupying the empty urban space opposite the Tyghuset. The study of the collections housed there is a fundamental premise to the architectural project. The Museum of Modern Art exhibits an excellent collection of Swedish painting and sculpture and examples of important avant-garde works from the 1950s, 1960s and 1970s. The Museum of Architecture exhibits a permanent collection on the history of architecture in Sweden, and houses an archive open to researchers and scholars. The buildings of the new museums establish a dialogue – light and discrete – with the fragmented surrounding context, without giving in to superfluous "monumentality". In accordance with this, the architecture proposed – discontinuous and interrupted – reflects the geography of the elements that compose the city of Stockholm, creating a picturesque, lively atmosphere that is far from artificial. The key component lies in the forms of the exhibit spaces, a composition of squares and rectangles in which the pyramidal ceiling provides both good illumination and adequate height. In visiting

Aerial view

the collection of paintings and sculpture at the Museum of Modern Art, an open gallery leads towards rooms located in compact blocks that allow a flexible presentation of the collection. The structure used for the gallery has precedents in the Dulwich Gallery (by John Soane), the MOCA in Los Angeles (by Arata Isozaki), the Portland Museum (by Ieoh Ming Pei) and in the enlargement of the National Gallery in London (by Venturi and Scott Brown). Access is through the walls of the Arrestbyggnaden, while the common entrance forces the visitor to choose between the two museums. The coatroom, toilets, storage areas, glass cases with information and entrance to the independent but necessary space for temporary exhibits are located next to the atrium, on the upper floor. In the back part is the café-restaurant that is turned towards the garden, where there are statues by Picasso, and it offers a splendid panoramic view of the sea and the city. In visiting the collection of paintings and sculpture at the Museum of Modern Art, an open gallery leads towards rooms located in compact blocks that allow a flexible presentation of the collection. The blocks of rooms are in contact with the exterior.

Skeppsholmen

One of the exhibit halls

Opposite page
above
View of one of the skylights
below
Sketch

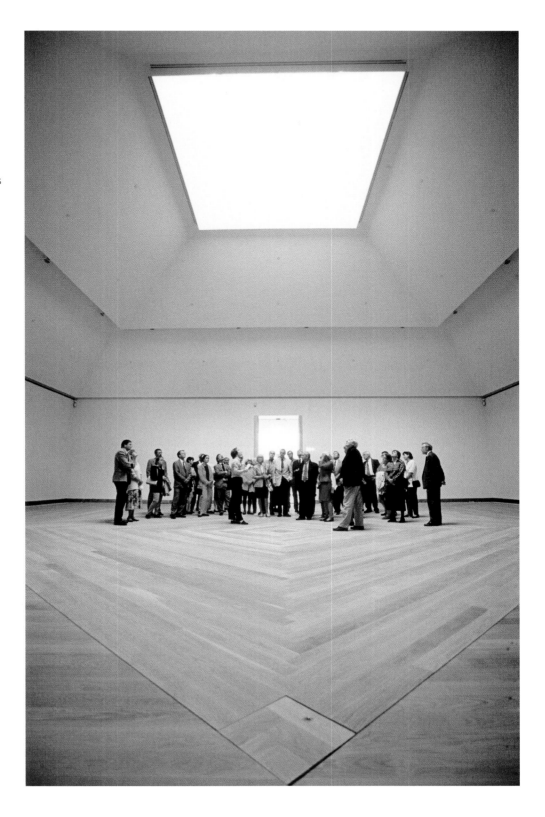

Julián Chivite Winery
Señorío de Arínzano, Spain 1991-2001

At the end of the 1980s, Chivite family bought property known as Señorío de Arínzano, located in the county of Aberin, in the Estello district. Señorío de Arínzano extends along both sides of the Ega River, along its bends, where the alluvial terrain rapidly becomes slopes that follow different orientations and that undulate and curve around, forming canals and escarpments from which one can contemplate the characteristic views of the Navarra, dominated by the silhouette of the Montejurra massif. Oak and royal oak are the typical species of the wooded areas, while along the banks of the river, there are poplars and ashwood, rush and blueberries. The past has left Señorío de Arínzano with some structures of singular interest: the Palace of the Commander of the Arsenal, a tower topped by statues sculpted in stone, a little church dedicated to St. Martin and an eighteenth century manor house. Inscribed in an 18x18-metre plot of land, the residence has undergone various modifications, and decisive intervention was taken in order to make it inhabitable and suitable for such a particular complex. Under the guidance of Julián Chivite and Fernando, Carlos and

Mercedes Chivite, who administer Señorío de Arínzano today, extensive work of rotation and improvement of the land was started up so that the grapevines could be planted without causing visible changes in the topography. In this landscape, the new winery was built keeping in mind that it is the culmination of the productive cycle. The new building is constituted of various annexes: a winery with an enclosed courtyard where the grapes are received; a quadrangular structure formed of five rooms for the pressing and processing; a pavilion that houses the containers for natural processing; a slightly sunken hall for the barrels where wines are stored. A separate building, with access on two levels, contains the bottling plant, offices, tasting rooms and commercial activities. The concrete walls of these buildings are worked so that they will acquire a patina similar to stone in a short time. For the roof structure and windows, oak was used, while the outside surface is in copper. The atmosphere created by these materials, the industrial elements that the production of wine requires and the oak barrels used contribute to the beginning of a positive dialogue among the elements.

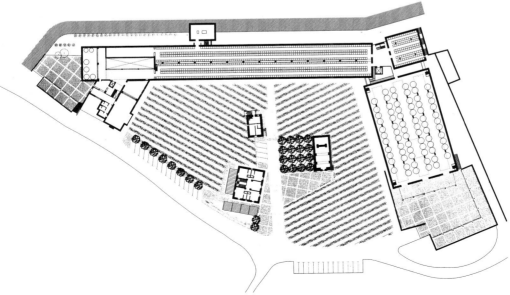

View of the space where
the *barriques* are housed

Opposite page
above
Aerial view
below
Ground plan

City Hall Extension
Murcia, Spain, 1992-1998

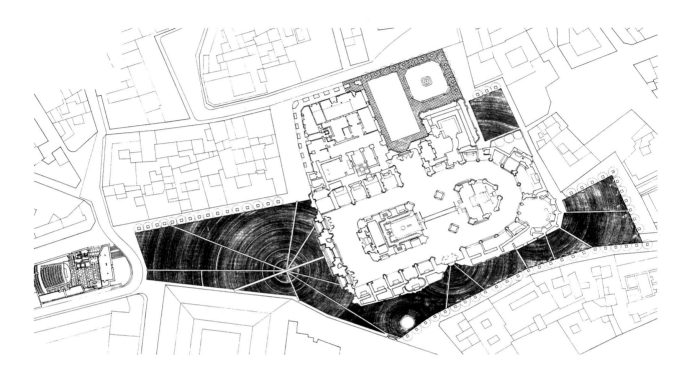

Ground plan of the site

Opposite page
View of the façade
in the city square

The new office building for the city of Murcia, in Cardenal Belluga Plaza, literally fills in a void that contributes to restoring the city square to its proper role.

The square still preserves the celebratory spirit of the Baroque style: as a consequence, it aims to design a building that can become a simple spectator, without taking on the role of protagonist, like on the other hand, the cathedral and the palace of Cardenal Belluga have.

Nevertheless, this is not just any spectator, since the building represents the civil power of the city.

In a space that recognizes, in the majestic façade of the cathedral and in the solemn front side of the Belluga palace, the importance that the church and its power in the eighteenth century, the future is present in a building that represents the authority of its citizens: the city hall.

In this way, a long-standing dispute has finally been resolved, since the city government, which only had its own building on the river available up to now, was ignorant of the city square, undoubtedly the most important urban in the city of Murcia. The façade of the new city hall is oriented towards the cathedral so as to give it the leading role in the life of the square, since from its strategic position, one can watch as various attractions take place there, and enjoy the splendid background of the façade of the religious building.

Yet the city hall does not have a door that opens on to the square, because its organization rigorously follows the geometry of the urban environment in which it is placed, which is not altered, but ennobled by the presence of the new building.

View of the main façade

View from the city hall looking out onto the square

The Audrey Jones Beck Building
The Museum of Fine Arts, Houston, USA, 1992-2000

Exhibition hall

The Museum of Fine Arts in Houston was built in 1924 after the design of the architect William Ward Watkin. Later, Mies van der Rohe built extensions in 1958 and then again in 1974. Mies's architecture was predominant, and today the first museum has been absorbed in the austere metallic structure of the German master.

The new construction, the Audrey Jones Beck Building, is separate and autonomous, but is connected to the museum proper through an underground gallery. The museum occupies a rectangular lot defined by Main Street, Fannin Street, Binz Avenue and Ewing Avenue. Despite the apparent homogeneity of the street grid, the study of the site drew attention to the

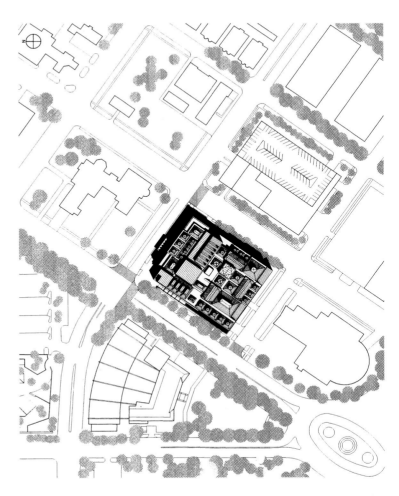

Plan/volumetrics of the site

following characteristics: the orientation of the building was the first decision in terms of design. The Audrey Jones Beck Building opens onto Main Street, which is thus its main orientation, not only because it is an important street for the city, but also because placing the main façade on this street is a tribute to the museum designed by Mies, thus establishing an indispensable relationship. Moreover, in Houston, buildings are perceived from the inside of an automobile, which makes it difficult to apply the same criteria as when considering an object with a well-defined image: in Houston it is not possible to have a frontal view of a building when travelling on foot. Such considerations led to having the Audrey Jones Beck Building occupy all of the land available. The site in Houston provided an opportunity to explore a compact kind of architecture. Building by maintaining restrictions imposed by the systematic nature of an area and including the largest possible volume in the smallest possible surface area were the aims strived for. It is possible to break a regular surface into a series of figures that define rooms and corridors, stairs and openings, galleries and courtyards, filling the space with continuity and contiguity, without a pre-established scheme, thus allowing

incredible compositional freedom. The Museum of Fine Arts in Houston is an example of this way of understanding architecture: the plan of the museum is broken up into a series of rooms connected by a hidden path that guides visitors and makes intense use of natural light, true protagonist of architecture whose essence is found in inner spaces.

Left
Exhibition hall with
zenithal lighting system

Below
Longitudinal section

Opposite page
View of the skylight
from below

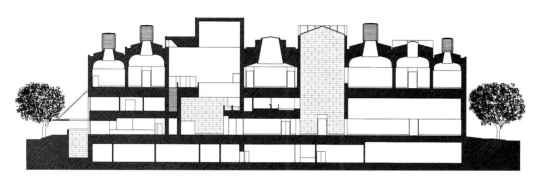

Royal and General Archives of Navarra
Pamplona, Spain, 1995-2003

Aerial view

The age-old Palace of the Kings of Navarra, built for King Sancho el Sabio at the end of the twelfth century, has become today's Archivo Real y General de Navarra. After it was abandoned by the army, the building continued to deteriorate and only the walls orientated towards the north and west remained intact. The design strategy was to intervene by conferring a renewed unity to the existing structures and to the newly built ones, marking the distinction between the various areas of the project – the archive on one side and the services on the other. Starting from the entrance, the visitor discovers the cloister, serving the two wings of the building. The hall housing documents is the west nave; in the north wind, the reading room; in the northwest corner, a staircase leads to the upper floors where, across a small area delimited by walls of the tower, one has access to the reading room. In the west wing, on the upper floors, there is space for a library for researchers. In the north wing, there are offices and conference rooms. The same functions are also housed in the south wing, to which some areas for the archiving of documents have been added. On the third floor are located service areas and laboratories for the conservation of documents. On the ground floor, a staircase leads to the

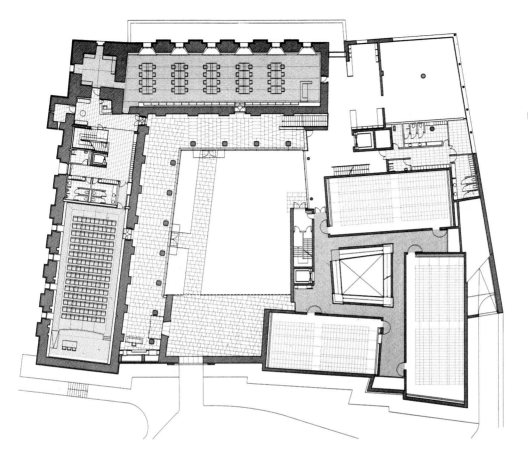

Plan of the ground floor

underground floor where there is a vaulted atrium, which best preserves the original nature of the artefact; it is used for temporary exhibits. The rooms of new construction, destined for the collection and conservation of documents, have been subdivided into several spaces, with the aim of avoiding an excessive concentration of archives. Archiving rooms have been arranged around the patio, entrusting the conjunction with the cloister to the vertical block of communication. When faced with the impossibility of recovering the entire construction, a radical solution to preserve existing ruins was adopted, covering them with a facing of new stone masonry that respected as far as possible the original characteristics. In this relation between new and old, it is worth mentioning the glassed-in area of the cloister: the destination of the use of the building and the desire to respect the contemporary nature of the project motivated the decision to cover it with glass: a transparent wall supported by a stainless steel structure.

From the heights of the high plain of Pamplona, the building appears as a unified, introverted complex that preserves the characteristic traits of the wall of the ancient Palace of the Kings, playing a fundamental role in defining the image of the city.

Left
General view
of the complex

Below
Section

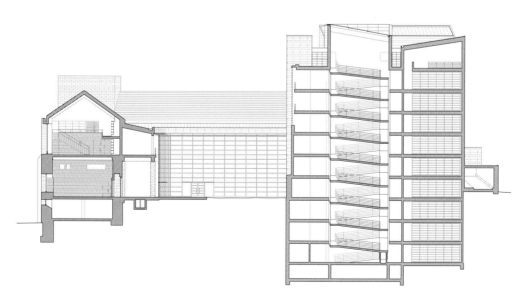

System of patio ramps
around which the archive
rooms are organized

The Prado Museum Extension
Madrid, Spain, 1995-2007

Entrance hall

The extension of the Prado Museum in the Jéronimos Cloister and the area behind the Museum should be understood as a new chapter in its long life. In this new stage of its existence the re-opening the Velázquez Entrance in the portico facing the Paseo del Prado enables the ascending spatial sequence which culminates in the Cloister of the Jéronimo. The original building has been liberated from all service functions that are not related to the exhibition of works of art, so that the museum's collections can be permanently hung in the galleries designed by Villanueva for the Academies. The transverse axis that starts in the portico and concludes in the cloister houses all ancillary, but nonetheless necessary activities, for the daily life of the Museum: the entrance spaces with the services required by the temporary galleries, the prints and drawings galleries and the laboratories for restoration of the works of art, etc.

The apse shaped hall on the ground floor, recalling Villanueva's design for the Basilica,

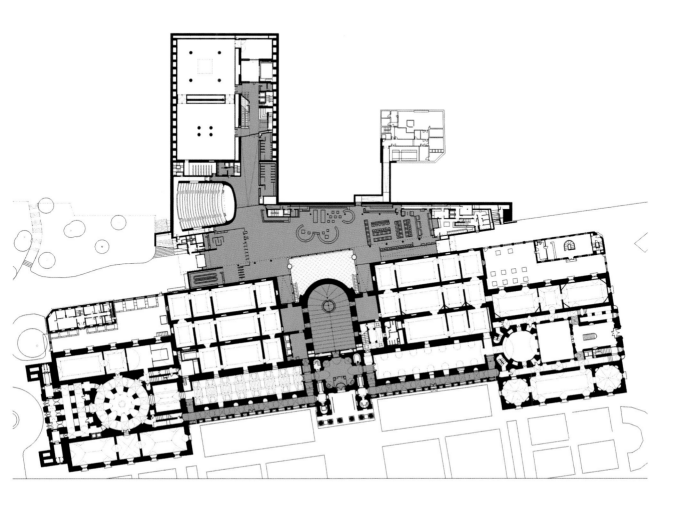

Plan of the new foyer

serves as the space in which the activities of the existing Prado Museum and the new extension overlap.

The new expansion has completely transformed the rear flank of the Museum. The imprecise and uncertain encounter that took place between the steep slope along Ruiz Alarcón Street and the walls of the volumes added on to the Museum over the years was transformed by erecting a platform planted with hedges covering the oblique space of the foyer. The garden mediates between the back of the Prado Museum and the new building surrounding the Cloister so that the Museum once again meets the slope that runs from the Buen Retiro to the Paseo del Prado in a way not very different from when Villanueva built the Academies. The terrace has been divided into parterres whose paths lead unavoidably to the apse of Villanueva highlighting what was the crux of not only this project, but most of the other interventions realized over the years in the history of the Museum.

Left
View of the cloister above
the new exhibition galleries

Below
Longitudinal section
through the cloister

Opposite page
Aerial view

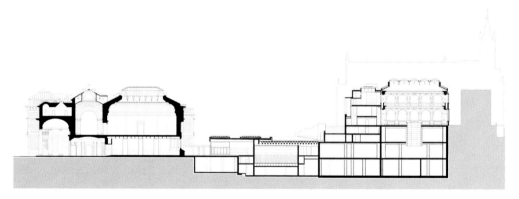

Our Lady of the Angels Cathedral
Los Angeles, California, USA, 1996-2002

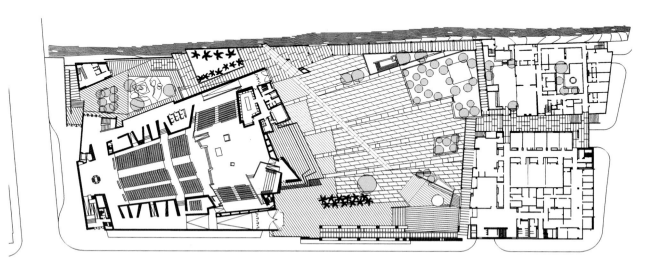

Ground plan of the site

"When I started to think about the Cathedral, I tried to remember works of modern architecture in which one could feel the presence of the sacred. The church in Turku by Erik Bryggman and Le Corbusier's chapel in Ronchamp came to mind – two contemporary churches that have most impressed me, and something they have in common is the importance of light. I see light as the protagonist of a space that tries to recover the sense of the transcendent, the vehicle through which we experience what we call sacred".

Thus Moneo indicates that light is at the origins if the Cathedral of Our Lady of the Angels. On the one hand, the light reflected from the chapels, captured by the large windows, leads us along the path towards the ambulatories that lead to the nave – light that is not very different from what we find in Romanesque churches. On the other, the light, filtered through alabaster creates a luminous, diffused and enveloping atmosphere in which the constructed elements "float", ensuring a spatial experience close to what we find in

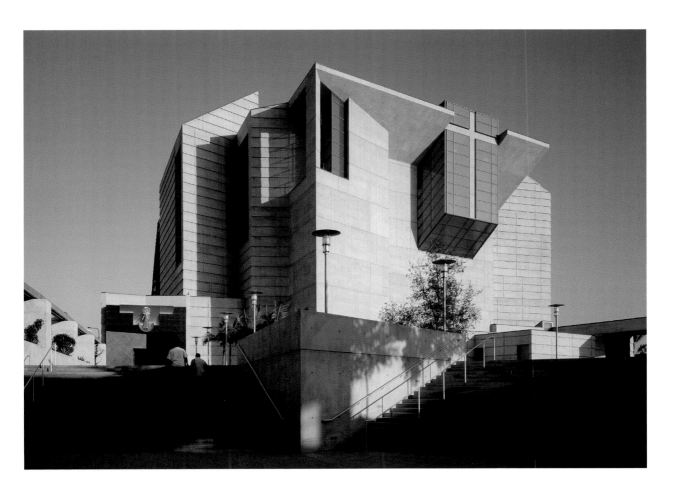

View of the building

different Byzantine churches. Finally, the glass cross that dominates the apse from on high lets us understand light as a mystic metaphor of the presence of God manifest in the rays of the sun that cross it, bringing about an architectural experience similar to the works of Baroque architects. The site of this new cathedral is in the city centre, and is tangential to the Hollywood Freeway, one of the major thoroughfares of the metropolis. Slightly elevated, the lot dominates the surroundings, emphasizing the role of the complex as an urban landmark and spiritual centre. It is an area that can hold up to six thousand people, and occupies the centre of the site with constructed volumes on both ends connected by colonnades that define the edges of the square. The cathedral is on the higher end, with its façade inclined slightly with respect to the long axis of the lot. The bell tower rises at the corner, separated from the church by a trapezoidal cloister that projects into the level ground in front of the church in the form of a little triangular lake lined with palm trees.

Above
View of the interior

Below
Longitudinal section

Opposite page
View of the liturgical hall

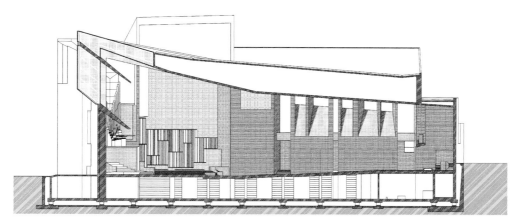

New Maternity Ward and Children's at Gregorio Marañón Hospital

Madrid, Spain, 1996-2003

View of the façade

The new maternity and paediatrics ward at Gregorio Marañón Hospital can be placed within the context of the reorganization of the complex into three "block types". A large square connects the old and new wings of the super-block under the parking area. The hospital occupies the entire part of the new construction. The main entrance is located in the transparent glass and aluminium body where there is access to both the maternity ward on the ground floor and the waiting room on the upper floors. The surrounding urban context influences the architecture of the building, which has a dense, compact formal structure on some of the floors. The rooms are – deliberately – all turned towards the patios in order to give a sense of isolation and tranquillity. The material used creates a mysterious, quiet atmosphere where light penetrates – discretely – the interior spaces. Within the perimeter where the spaces supporting medical activity are located, the building shows how flexible it is by adapting to the urban context. The "two hospitals" have different, independent accesses on two different floors. There is a common connecting

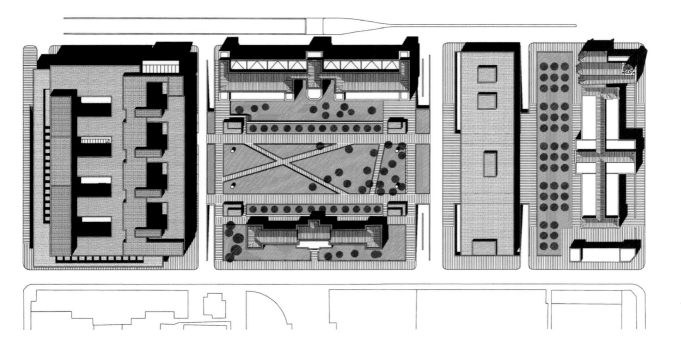

floor, and general services are located there. The supporting structure in reinforced concrete, both in slabs as well as in vertical faces, contributes to perfect sound insulation. Dividers in multi-layered plasterboard are arranged to make the structure agile and capable of holding medical machinery. The marble of the floors and the baseboard of the corridors protect against intense use these spaces get. The grès and coloured linoleum – used in the areas subject to humidity – make the ambient warm and hygienic thanks to the absence of joins. The frames of the windows and blinds, both in maple wood, give the rooms an atmosphere of familiarity by trying to avoid the customary austere image of the hospital environment. The attic is equipped for proper conservation of the machinery, which is extremely important within a hospital structure. The choice of vitreous material both in the patios as well as on the exterior gives the entire structure a salubrious, sophisticated image. English-style patios, frameworks and urban structures are all in granite, thus guaranteeing continuity of the building with respect to the original structure from which the project was developed.

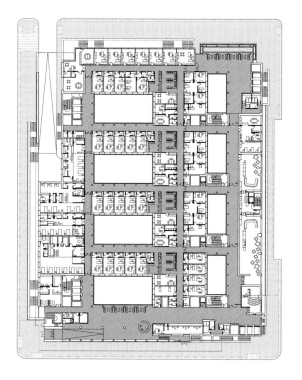

Above
View of an interior

Left
Plan of the ground floor
and view of the inner
courtyard from inside
a room

Opposite page
View of one of the inner
courtyards

Library, Arenberg Campus
Leuven, Belgium, 1997-2002

Site plan

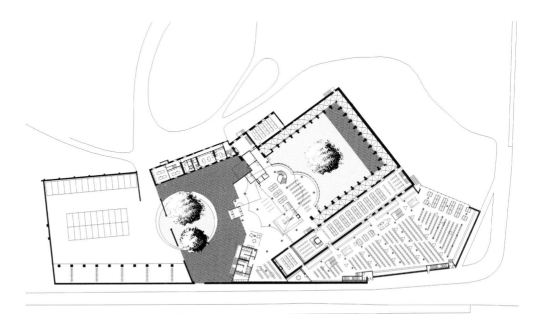

In 1997 the ruins of the Celestine Convent floated around like a ship adrift between the roads and highways connecting the city of Leuven with its surroundings. New roads had been superimposed on the old ones and the ship without a mast, once a monastery, appeared to have gone off course, making it difficult to understand the importance of the ruins of the cloister.

With the disappearance of the church, only three sides of the convent remained, together with a chapter house and a wing of residential buildings. Imposing trees along the perimeter of the convent gave the impression of a farm resting on a gentle slope. Ever since he began the study, Moneo wanted to maintain the scale and the character of the place by making the minuscule cloister the central nucleus of the new library. The design strategy called for a building that was neither high nor mimetic to enclose the cloister, the reconstruction of which led to the discovery of a new, unexpected space: a covered courtyard was placed beside the cells of the monks and the walls of the old annexes of the monastery, in counterpoint to the cloistered monastery.

The organic geometry of the new construction gives strength and life to the austere convent by offering time a friendly gesture of welcome in the entrance courtyard, to which one has access both from the hill path as well as from the street. The use of the ground floor and the desire to maintain the building at a minimal height made it obligatory to locate the book storage areas in the basement of the new construction and the shelves in the basement and on the ground floor, which extends on horizontal planes between the pre-existent brick walls that face the street and the reading room of the former refectory annexed to the convent. The result of this strategy is that the existent volumes preserve their value while the roof of the old refectory continues to be the most visible element.

The old monastery is a building that was salvaged and recently reintegrated in the life of the city and of the university. The prayers of the monks have given way to the blinking monitors of computers, and the lively conversations of students have become the alternative to the choral chanting of the Celestine community.

General view of the building in relation to pre-existing structures

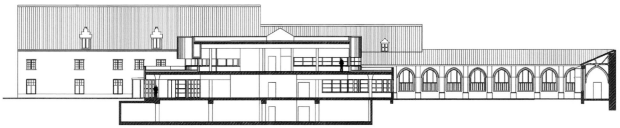

Above
Graft of the new building
onto pre-existing structure

Below
Longitudinal section

Opposite page
Interiors

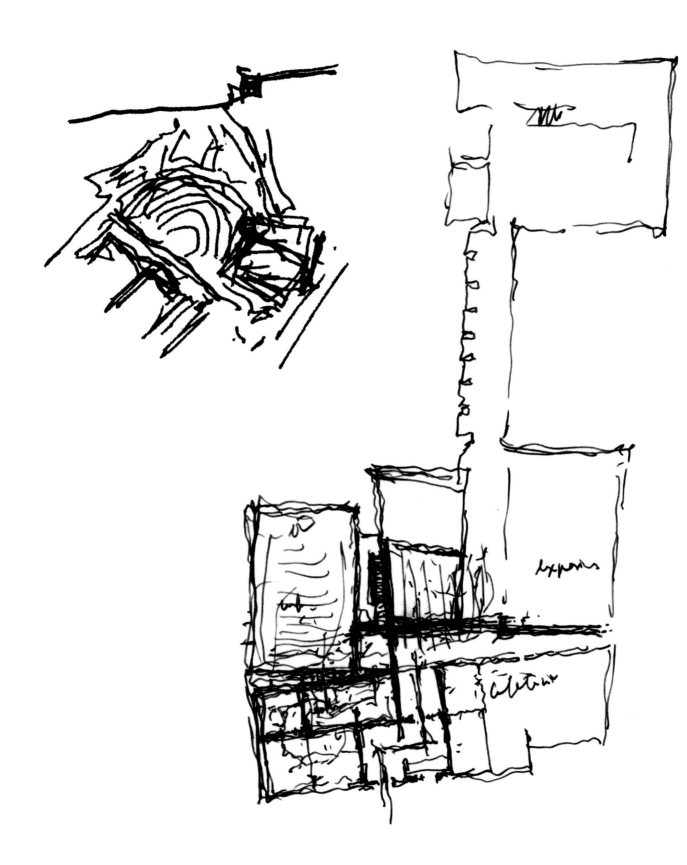

Projects

Roman Theater of Cartagena Museum
Cartagena, Spain, 2001 (park), 2002 (museum)

Model

The discovery and excavation of the Roman Theater of Cartagena these past years has been a most important event in the rich archaeological history of the city. It has brought to light an exceptional monument. The fact that the remains of the ancient theater have not appeared until now can be explained by their location in a part of the city that has been occupied without interruption since pre-Roman times. The re-use of the site as a market in the Byzantine period, and the erection, probably in the second half of the 13th century, of the Church of Santa María la Vieja on top of the upper part of the theate illustrate the intricate concatenation of constructions that make this area of the city a true lesson in history.

We could say that the aim of the intervention has been to make the Roman Theater part of the city by connecting pre-existing buildings and voids in the urban framework, thereby creating a museum-like route that leads the visitor from the lower levels of the port up to the summit, where we find the old cathedral and the theater.. The museum 'promenade' flows through exhibition spaces lit by a complex system of skylights, and includes escalators as well as elevators that act as frames through which to present the pieces found by archaeologists during the course of the excavation.

The museum is articulated into two distinct buildings united by a corridor under the street: the first building, which incorporates the existing bays of the Palazzo di Riquelme, is organized around an impluvium court. The second one houses the exhibition galleries, as well as the vertical circulations taking the visitors up to the level of the corridor that was lies under the remains of the Santa María la Vieja church leading visitors up to the theater. It is perhaps the double reading that can be made of the intervention – museum complex and archaeological garden blended into the city – that contributes most to making the project one of interest.

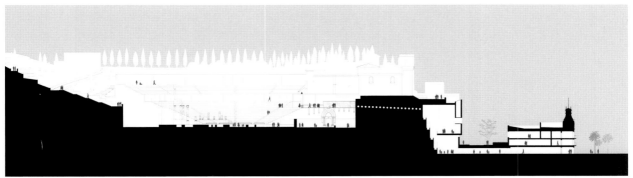

Above
Aerial view of the Roman theater

Below
Longitudinal section

Columbia University Northwest Science Building

New York, Usa, 2005-2010

The building was commissioned by Columbia University in 2005. Located in the northwest corner of the historic Morningside campus, It will be completed by the end of 2010 providing over 15,000 square metres of physics and chemistry laboratories as well as classrooms, a lounge and cafeteria, a new entrance to the gymnasium, a 4,500 square metre library, and a 170 seat auditorium. The main objective of the project was to develop a system of connections between the existing grid of streets and the campus area in a site strongly conditioned by an existing structure, the Francis S. Levien Gymnasium, not to mention the desire and effort not to change – and hence to respect as far as possible – the main lines of the masterplan designed by McKim, Mead & White in 1987.

Consequently, the volume of the building was forced from the outset – according to the limits imposed by the original plan and current building programme – to fit within a gap of barely two meters between adjacent laboratory buildings as well as to heighten the dense character of the campus. This goal and the technical difficulties connected with it were overcome with a daring structural solution that would enable the building to be suspended over the gymnasium by means of a "bridge building" spanning over 42 metres. The Broadway façade of the complex, characterised by the visible structural framework covered with panels of aluminium and glass arranged according to a rigorous geometry, forms a texture of light and shadow through which the mass of the building appears as a vibrant volume supported by a sculptural pedestal in stone. The compact body of the building suspended over the gym makes it possible for the entrance spaces, situated on the inner level of the campus, and the library spaces enjoy views onto Broadway. Moreover, its intrinsic transparency allows for views through the building. Consequently the façade facing toward the inside of the campus is almost entirely glazed so as to reveal the functions and activities going on inside the complex and to help achieve the desired openness and interaction with the campus.

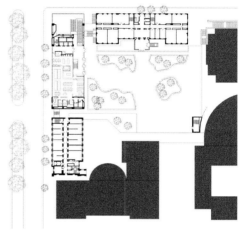

Renders and site plan

Church (The Iesu) in Riberas de Loyola
Donostia-San Sebastián, Spain, 2009

Right
View toward the cross

Below
Site plan

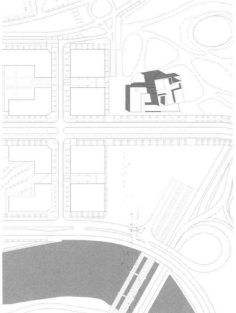

The church for the diocese of Donastia-San Sebastian is a different experience for the architect after the large scale of the Cathedral of Los Angeles. On this occasion the goal of the architecture was primarily to help configure a space capable of contributing to the life of the community that feels Christian in the midst of a plural and diverse society. The parish came into being with a will to serve at the entrance to a new residential district Riberas de Loyola located along the bend of the Urumea River that establishes continuity with the city through its park. The new building, a tall, massive, cubic volume constituting the main body of the church is organized around a small interior court overlooked by a meeting room, classrooms and apartments for the priests and visitors. A supermarket in the lower level closely connected to the park, is understood as a meeting place: an up to date version of the open markets under porticos. The church space is a compact body hollowed out on the corners so as to delineate a cross. The cross appears again in the roof, bringing in a perimeter of light that is in an attempt to use once again the metaphor that leads us to understand light as a manifestation of transcendence.

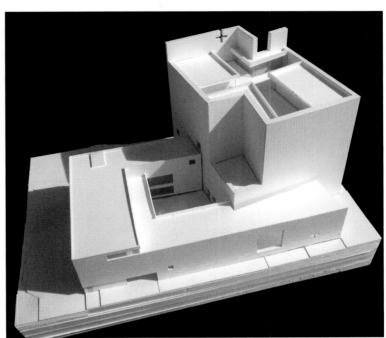

Models and plan

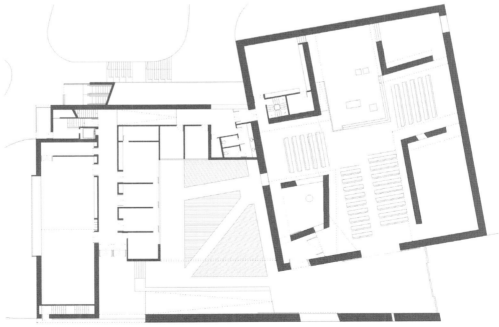

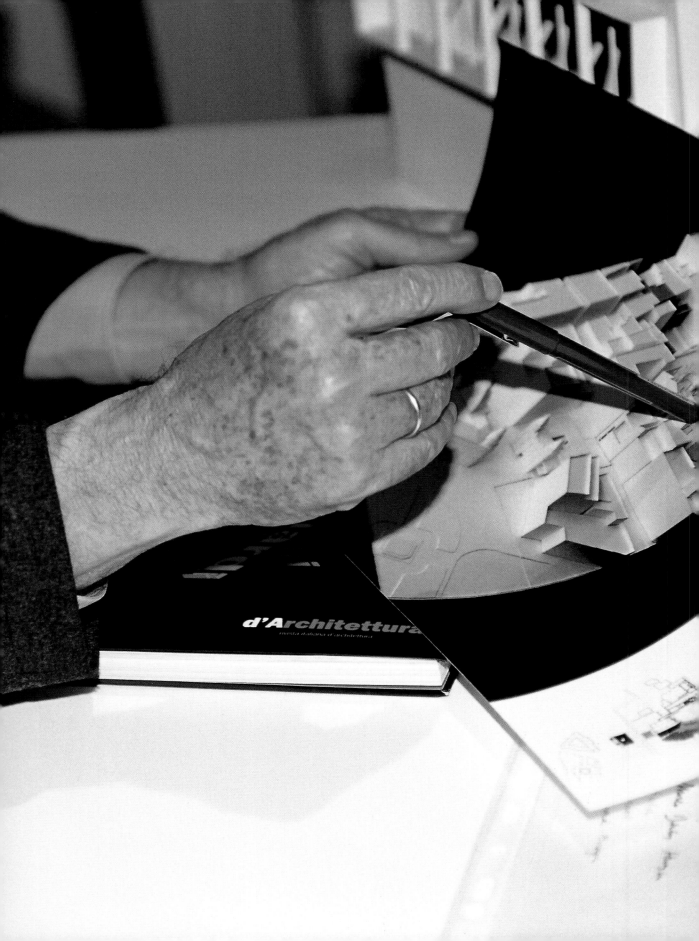

d'Architettura
rivista italiana d'architettura

Thought

The Solitude of Buildings

I thank Dean McCue for his kind words. Once again, I understand the responsibilities I have inherited in accepting the chairmanship of the Department of Architecture of the Harvard University Graduate School of Design, starting July 1st. I cannot forget those who have led the school in the past; but permit me to confess how much it touches me to know that I will hold the position once held by the late Josep Lluis Sert. This is the greatest stimulus, and at the same time, a great challenge. I expect and hope that he will act as my remote and loved mentor.

I felt honored when Dean McCue asked that I become a candidate for this position, and was understandably assailed by fears about its commitments and duties, because I realize what Harvard means: people all over the world look to Harvard as their guide.

With the awareness that Dean McCue and Professor Harry Cobb would be beside me, I accepted the position, certain that I would find here at the GSD the enthusiastic and competent faculty able to carry out the work implicit in the school's pedagogic mission.

I firmly wish to serve the school in striving toward the four qualities Professor Cobb identified five years ago when he accepted the position I will hold, and I quote him now: "The qualities that seem essential to our educational mission are coherence, rigour, openness and audacity." I know how much Dean McCue and Professor Cobb have endeavoured to emphasize these qualities at the school. Openness and audacity, coherence and rigour. I could not find better words to define the future of the school as I envision it. That is my firm belief and I will work to keep these qualities as alive as they are today. Let me affirm that I will not disappoint those who have placed their confidence in me. The one statement I am able to make at this early date is a promise. I will do my best and put all my energy into serving the university, honoring what some universities have professed and what I still believe: that knowledge is not the private property of one group of people or one country, and that it should be shared by all people of good will throughout the world.

On a different note, it is a duty for me, as much as a pleasure, to present myself and my work to the students and my fellow faculty members tonight. I would like to thank the GSD and the endowment given in the name of Kenzo Tange for this opportunity.

I have chosen three buildings as examples of my work. They differ with respect to requirements and site conditions, but all are public buildings. They may be regarded as representative of my work over the last ten years.

Why buildings instead of projects? Why work instead of a theoretical discourse? I believe that in the crude reality of built works one can see clearly the essence of a project, the consistency of ideas. I firmly believe that architecture needs the support of matter; that the former is inseparable from the latter. Architecture arrives when our thoughts about it acquire the real condition that only materials can provide. By accepting and bargaining with limitations and restrictions, with the act of construction, architecture becomes what it really is.

I know these words may sound odd today. First, because we are in a school of architecture where learning is based upon the convention implied by drawings and models. We are therefore inclined to believe that within these resides the entire discipline. Second, because during the last, let me say fifteen years, many architects have believed that construction is not worth the effort it involves. For them the task was finished at the drawingboard, avoiding any contamination. And fears of contamination are understandable. Architecture as a profession is a long way from satisfying anyone who loves the discipline. It has lost the importance that it had in society in the past. Victor Hugo said that books had killed cathedral architecture; it wasn't entirely true then, but it seems we could say today that mass media communication has reduced architecture's relevance. Architecture is no longer vital neither as in the most pragmatic point of view that identifies it with cities and housing or as the reservoir of symbolic communication. Architects unconsciously recognize this problem but are not willing to confront it directly. And therefore, although they would like to connect architecture with society and reality as in the past, they often take a wrong path and become prophets of utopian dreams. Architects desire a bigger role for architecture, or at least a more respected position. And perceiving it unreachable, we architects are protecting ourselves by nurturing the fantasy that architecture can be represented simply through drawings. Such a view has been supported by the dialectic between utopia and reality. If architects cannot serve reality, they at least will work for the future world dreamed of in utopia. Such a view has produced beautiful drawings and presented wonderful intentions, but in my opinion these efforts are not intrinsically architecture – which does not mean that people who act this way are not architects.

I realize how predominant this approach is today, but at the same time architects must resent this approach, because buildings begin to appear as mere reflections of drawings or as direct physical representations of a process. This dramatically changes the relationship between the buildings and reality. Many architects today invent processes or master drawing techniques without concern for the reality of building. The tyranny of drawings is evident in many buildings when the builder tries to follow the drawing literally. The reality belongs to the drawing not to the building. There are so many examples of this attitude that I do not need to elaborate it. The buildings refer so directly to the architect's definition and are so unconnected with the operation of building that the only reference is the drawing. But a truly architectural drawing should imply above all the knowledge of construction. Today many architects ignore issues about how a work is going to be built. Some will argue this has happened in the past that some works were executed without being visited by their architects, who trusted directly in drawings and specifications for the execution of their projects. But, of course, everyone will agree that architects in the past benefited from a social coherence that does not exist today. A drawing accepted, before it was drawn, certain building conventions. It has been only recently, perhaps with some architects of the Enlightenment that the connection between graphic expression and building knowledge began to dissolve.

On the other hand, many architects believe that the work of architecture should entail the exact registration of a process. If in the 1920s the idea of *promenade architecturale* transformed the building structure and produced a series of sequences that introduced the idea of movement, in the 1980s the idea of architecture as the physical conclusion that consolidates a mental process has taken its place. By this transformation of a mental process in the consolidated reality, the self-expression of a building becomes less important than the expression of the architect's thoughts. Moreover, the automatic nature of the production of architecture prevents the object's autonomy. And, naturally, questions arise: Can the process be considered the aim of architecture? Doesn't architecture lie in the production of something else? May the simple registration of the process become the reality that we call architecture? Are buildings simply three-dimensional translations of drawings or the outcome of a so-called process? Previously this was not the case, when architects thought first of the reality of buildings and later of the drawings with which they might describe these thoughts. Today the terms of this relationship are often inverted.

The result of this conflict with physical reality is that architecture is transformed immediately either into the reflection of drawing or the representation of process. The word that best characterizes the most distinctive feature of academic architecture today is "immediateness". Architecture tries to be direct, immediate, the simple dimensional extension of drawings. Architects want to keep the flavor of their drawings. And if this is their most desired goal, in so wishing architects reduce architecture to a private, personal domain. It follows that this immediateness transforms the intentions of the architect; and turns what should be presumed as general into a personal, expressionist statement. Architecture has lost its necessary contact with society and, as a result, has become a private world.

Can architecture be a private world? May it be reduced to a personal expression? Architects, as much as they admire the personal realm in which other artists seem to work, do not work under the same conditions. In my opinion, their work should be shared by others, or at least, it should not be so personal as to invade the public realm in a manner that no longer belongs naturally to the sphere of the public environment. Architecture itself implies public involvement from the specific moment at which the design process starts until construction ends. And again we are on slippery ground, because the boundaries between public and private worlds today are more blurred than ever. When architecture is produced in cities, it conveys a public idea. Cities have a need for an architecture that is both a tool, in the sense of artificially transforming the physical environment, and a frame for supporting social life. The notion of a shared language for producing the world of objects — the different types of buildings in and with which we live — emerges as a given for understanding architecture and its production. And therefore I do not think that we can justify as architecture the attempts of some artists who, confusing our discipline with any three-dimensional experience, create unknown objects that at times relate to a natural mimesis, and at other times allude to unusable machines.

But without the connection that existed in the past between project and production, builders become mere instruments, and technique becomes subjugated — a slave. The intimacy between architecture and construction has been broken. This intimacy was once the very nature of the architectural work and somehow was always manifested in its appearance. We know that a deterministic discourse doesn't explain architecture, but we admit that architects should accept techniques and use building systems for starting the process of the formal invention that ends in architecture. Even architecture such as Le Corbusier's should be seen in the light of the time-honored acceptance of building technologies as the base for the formal proposal. And to be an architect, therefore, has traditionally implied being a builder; that is, explaining to others how

to build. The knowledge (when not the mastery) of the building techniques was always implicit in the idea of producing architecture. The knowledge of construction principles should be so thorough as to allow the architect the formal invention that always precedes the fact of the construction itself. It should appear as if the techniques imposed have come to accept form's boundaries, for it is the acknowledgement of these limits that renders so explicit the presence of building procedures in architecture. Paradoxically, it is technical flexibility that allows architects to forget the presence of technique. The flexibility of today's techniques has resulted in their disappearance, either in architecture itself or in the process of thinking about it. This is something new. Architects in the past were both architects and builders. Before the present disassociation, the invention of form was also the invention of its construction. One implied the other.

Architecture has always presented inherent arbitrariness as something unobtrusive. In other words, arbitrariness of form disappeared in construction, and architecture acted as the bridge between the two. Today arbitrariness of form is evident in the buildings themselves, because construction has been dealt out of the game of design. When arbitrariness is so clearly visible in the buildings themselves, architecture is dead; what I understand as the most valuable attribute of architecture disappears.

The price of such an attitude is paid by architecture, because very often some architects present us with an image of fragility and with a taste for the fictional. This is the natural consequence of immediateness. Curiously, this did not happen with the architecture of the Modern Movement, where the idea of immediateness could not be applied. Whether we are considering the techniques or the social goals, the architects of the Modern Movement respected both techniques and building programs. While their architecture perhaps was not successful in solving the problems posed simultaneously, they strove to involve such concerns in their work, and consequently their architecture cannot be characterized by its immediateness. Then, the idea of architecture always implied an awareness of the outside world in addition to the strength of the images. But today the lack of contact with the outside world brings with it the fantasy of an autonomous architecture controlled exclusively on the drawing board.

It may be argued that architecture in the future will lack the quasi-perennial condition that it had in the past and will from now on be characterized as ephemeral. That would explain the tenuous condition of our buildings despite their stone. Architecture is influenced today by this ephemeral condition and thus presents itself as ephemeral, no matter what its material. And this poses for us a major question: Is architecture today no longer able to endure as it did in the past? In today's architecture does there exist the sensation that works are perishable? I think these questions must be answered affirmatively, and only in so doing will we be able to oppose such a tendency, by acknowledging the gratifying way in which buildings accepted their own lives in the past. The construction of a building entails an enormous amount of effort and a major investment. Architecture in principle, almost by economic principle, should be durable. Materials should provide for the building's long life. A building formerly was built to last forever or, at least we certainly did not expect it to disappear. But today things have changed. Although we resist regarding our architecture this way, it is far removed from traditional architecture, despite our professed respect for history. We probably unconsciously know that architecture is not going to last as long as it used to. But we reject such ideas, even though the real situation affects architecture and marks it with the flavor of the ephemeral. If architecture is ephemeral it can be immediate.

If architecture once contributed to the reality of fiction, henceforth it will contribute to the fiction of fiction. The pride of architecture was to make real the fiction, because the way in which architecture was produced implied continuity between form, as contrived in the mind, and built form in such a way that the latter became the only existing reality. The ideal world was transformed into a real world because what characterized architecture was the fact that it should be built. It was a mental product that took its consistency from the act of expression alone, becoming at the same time an independent reality. Today's architecture has lost contact with its genuine supports, and immediateness is the natural consequence of this critical change suffered by the role of architecture in the world. I still believe in an architecture of reality, but I should acknowledge the great extent to which my belief is the manifestation of a wish for more than what I can reasonably forecast for the future.

I do not think this is the appropriate moment to discuss further such important concerns, but in my opinion these discussions should take place in the school, and I would like to pursue these issues with interested students. Nonetheless I would like to respond to some of the questions I have introduced. Architects should realize that architecture, the work in which they are involved, their work, is a complex reality including many presences; for this reason the immediateness-fantasy is not possible. All these presences are reflected in the multiple mirror that a building is. They should be acknowledged in the design operation, in order to avoid the reduction that always distorts architectural reality. The fact that architects may become aware of the many ways in which their work is limited, that it has real boundaries ranging from the ideology to the brick, does not preclude architecture from being rendered. The ability to accommodate the multiple presences inherent in buildings should be the key with which the architect condenses disparity into the single self-supported presence of buildings.

As much as I consider drawings and models the necessary and natural support for our discussions about architecture in school, I encourage students to understand the immense pleasure that the actual production of architecture, the construction of buildings, offers. This means that I would like to accompany students in their initiation as architects, to be beside them, as they become makers of buildings. We are living in a discontinuous world – in times of uncertainty, as Professor Cobb likes to say – and architects, regardless of their wishes and intentions, suffer as they stand unprotected before the diversity of the society in which they work. Therefore, once the architect has acquired his or her skills, the training of his or her eyes, the first imperative is to gain the critical knowledge that will permit the choice of the coordinates within which his or her career will develop; these are the coordinates to which his or her buildings will refer.

An architectural initiation includes today, in my opinion, a strong familiarity with history – a history that is no longer a storehouse of forms or a workshop of styles, but one that simply offers the material for thinking about the evolution of architecture, as well as the way in which architects worked in the past.

Now, why do I insist so much on the conviction that buildings are neither the outcome of a process nor the materialization of a drawing? In other words, why do I insist on the idea that buildings are not the exclusive property of the architect? Mainly because I believe the presence of the architect quickly disappears and that, once completed, buildings take on a life of their own. Architects endure all the difficulties involved in raising buildings – artifacts that perhaps at first can be said to reflect our intentions, express our desires and represent the problems we discuss in schools. For a time, we regard our buildings as mirrors; in their reflection we recognize who we are, and eventually who we were. We are tempted to think that a building is a personal statement within the ongoing process of history; but today I am certain that once the construction is finished, once the building assumes its own reality and its own role, all those concerns that occupied the architects and their efforts dissolve. There comes a time when buildings do not need protection of any kind, neither from the architects nor from the circumstances. In the end, circumstances alone remain as hints, allowing critics and historians to gain knowledge of the buildings and to explain to others how they took their form.

The building itself stands alone, in complete solitude – no more polemical statements, no more troubles. It has acquired its definitive condition and will remain alone forever, master of itself. I like to see the building assume its proper condition, living its own life. Therefore, I do not believe that architecture is just the superstructure that we introduce when we talk about buildings. I prefer to think that architecture is the air we breathe when buildings have arrived at their radical solitude.

Are all these considerations present in our works? I would like them to be. Because when architects realize that a building masters its own life, their approach to design is different; it changes radically. Our personal concerns become secondary and the final reality of the building becomes the authentic aim of our work. It is the building's materiality, its own being that becomes the unique and exclusive concern. This attitude allows us to establish the necessary distance between the building and ourselves.

Of all the figurative or plastic arts, architecture is probably the one in which the distance between the artist and his work is the greatest. A painter or a sculptor may leave his or her own direct imprint on the canvas or the stone; he or she often is inextricably attached to his or her work. This does not happen in architecture. In our discipline a natural distance separates us from our work; this distance should always be maintained, especially when our thoughts start to be materialized in a project. To keep this distance is to acknowledge architectural reality, but it is also the precondition for beginning a project. Architecture implies distance between our work and ourselves, so that in the end the work remains alone, self-supported, once it has acquired its physical consistency. Our pleasure lies in the experience of this distance, when we see our thought supported by a reality that no longer belongs to us. What is more, a work of architecture, if successful, may efface the architect.

Are all these thoughts present in the work I will now present? I believe they were my companions throughout time. I fought hard to give Bankinter the splendor that baked clay may acquire when used in urban fabric, in this way establishing a

natural connection with the existing villa. I tried to reflect the presence of the public realm in the city when I designed Logroño.
I hoped the Roman world would once again be alive in Mérida, a Roman city that had almost lost its memory. (Courtesy of Rafael Moneo)

The "Kenzo Tange Lecture", a commemorative lecture sponsored by the Harvard University Graduate School of Design was given by Rafael Moneo when he accepted the post of Chairman of the Department of Architecture. The lecture was given on March 9, 1985, in George Gund Hall.

David Cardelús

Kursaal, San Sebastián 1999
p. 94

Ana Muller

Atocha Station, Madrid 1992
pp. 96-97

Lluís Casals

Diagonal, Barcelona 1993
pp. 98-99

Åke E:son Lindman

View of Stockholm, 1997
pp. 100-101

Duccio Malagamba

Julián Chivite Winery, Señorío de Arínzano 2002
pp. 102-103

Kursaal, San Sebastián 1999
pp. 108-109

Roland Halbe

Auditorium, Barcelona 1999
p. 104

Eugeni Pons

Auditorium, Barcelona 2000
p. 105

Timothy Hursley

Our Lady of the Angels Cathedral, Los Angeles
pp. 106-107

Photographers

Critique

Consciousness and the Need for Knowledge

Josep Quetglas
The dance and the procession
The form of time in the architecture
of Rafael Moneo

Men take multiple paths. Whoever follows them and compares them will see strange figures appear – figures that seem to belong to the great writing in code that we see everywhere: on the wings of birds, on eggshells, in the clouds and in the snow, in crystals and in rock formations, on ice-covered waters, in the inner and outer structures of mountains, plants, animals and human beings, in the stars in the sky, on slabs of pitch and of glass when we touch them after having scratched their surfaces or in the filings around a magnet, in strange coincidences. In them, we guess at the key to this singular writing and its grammar, but this premonition does not seem to want to submit to any definite form…
Novalis, *The Disciples in Thaïs*

Writing on Rafael Moneo: it is like trying to grasp the meaning of the writing in code that crosses any work; like thinking you can understand a foreign word pronounced out loud; like groping around in a purse to find out what is inside. It is useless.

The difficulty – the pretentiousness – of this attempt does not only reside in daring to decode a work by means of an interpretation, in daring to pursue a practice with words. In the case of many like me, it is also necessary to add the following: the words used by those among us who did not pass through the Faculty of architecture in Barcelona in the 1960s and 1970s come from Rafael Moneo. It was he who manufactured them; we owe our ability to speak (that is to say, to see and imagine) to him. Perhaps we are ready to dig into any work except the one we have remained in and that contains us.

I would like to say that the work of an architect with such an important role in the teaching and training of others is, in the first place, in his architecture and then in the way in which his teaching brought them to understand architecture. In a certain imprecise way, nonetheless, it is also contained in all of us who, heterogeneous, mediocre, irregular, hindered, in no way heirs, in no

way effective use words in the sense that we thought we had learned from Rafael Moneo. Moreover, there a "final paradox"[1]: everything that those of us who assume the condition of epigones say or write consists of reiterated delay, in slow preparation.

It is as if, in the immense parabola that is forming our lives, all of our activity were becoming oriented according to learning that could one day allow us to talk about Rafael Moneo.

One day I will write on Rafael Moneo. But not now. For the moment, I think I possess only disconnected threads, fragments of descriptions, a few projects, some more credible than others, notes taken from his writings or lectures. One day, I would like that it all should become part of an overall interpretation of his work, but for the moment it does not create a credible portrait, not even remotely. Vast white spaces remain among the projects, while I have no idea as to what to say about entire projects.

The passages that I have collected refer for the most part to time. I think I understand that the form of time in the architecture of Rafael Moneo is an excellent tool to grasp the key, because I think that his architecture puts forward a different kind of temporality than that of most architects. This is the specific trait in which Moneo is discreetly explained and described to us, in which "la arquitectura, el mundo formal que nos rodea, puede ser eficaz bisturí para cogenza a desentrañar la situation mental de una determinada epoca"[2].

[…]

In the case of both Rossi and Moneo, Form manages to become stable only after building a dam against the tempests of open time, to fluctuate in the basin of the past or in Messianic time. In both cases, we contemplate architecture with the same tenderness towards inevitable failure that Marguerite Duras describes in *Un barrage contre le Pacifique*. How weak and emotional were those fragile, unnatural palisades of earth and bamboo with which the mother of the narrator tried to protect the form of the beloved cultivated fields from the ocean, from monsoons, from uncommon weather, which the first gust of wind would have blown away without any obstacles.

In Rafael Moneo, there is a different proposal. There is no cooling down in time, nor is there flight. In order to preserve form, he does not try to separate it, but instead incorporates time inside, adopting it as constituent material of the work itself.

[…]

Some of Rafael Moneo's projects dance, while others move in procession.

Those that dance inaugurate their own time and space, depending only on their body, and they use the dancer as the origin and reference for every measure. The body is not inscribed in a system of previous coordinates, unless it is to immediately cancel out at the first gesture and articulate from that point onwards the imminence and eruption of their own new – and forever initial – spatiality and temporality. This is how it is with the Bankinter and the city hall in Logroño. Fortunately, they have been described on the basis of their composition in the layout, sustained by the diagonal. The diagonal is in line with whatever moves. The fan, the figure of movement in whatever dance, gathers all of the diagonals possible into a bunch.

But there are also projects by Rafael Moneo that move in procession. The procession is not a slow, unidirectional, monodic dance. On the contrary, it is the opposite of dance. The procession gathers time – it does not invent it, nor disperse it – it accumulates time in the basin of its gestures and marks it. Without procession, time would continue to flow, but inaudibly, invisibly.

Like a drum head, the procession projects a beat that is not only its own; it amplifies it and gives it meaning. In the procession, two temporalities coincide, and this is their emotion: the random, fleeting and adventurous time of the bodies and steps of the celebrants, and at the same time, a deep beat, a deaf drum: the time of the world. Some of Rafael Moneo's projects make it audible because inside them, as in a drum shell, they cultivate the beat.

[…]

In Stockholm, Moneo impresses an arrangement on the room that "is not processional, but rather a labyrinth". Unity appears all of a sudden, without any one pavilion taking priority over another, like the rumbling in the ground of "simultaneous bubbles of rain". "The discontinuous structure of the city is present in the building, and that determines the way in which one moves in the rooms." In talking about this project, Moneo put forward, between the museum in Stockholm and the project for the block on Avenida Diagonal in Barcelona, a comparison that originated in the different conditions of luminosity in the two cities: the quality of the light, the duration of a single source, the sun's motion "around" the Earth, that is, time. "In Barcelona, I try to capture transversal, momentary light", of which the rear parts of the building that capture or produce and prolong the grooved shadows, in the same way in which the iron parts of Sol LeWitt's balustrades make the shadow of a virtual bas-relief adhere to the flat surface of a façade, or the differences between the facing in polished or opaque stone is not limited to guaranteeing conservation. "In Stockholm, instead, light lasts a long time. Here the project is a work with profiles. The museum is seen as a group of dark masses in the mysterious light that appears after the sun has gone down. A light that emanates from the shadows of objects."

The light that appears after the sun has disappeared over the horizon, when, that is to say, time cannot be measured. What other kind of illumination is possible to present objects that do not want to be measured, that do not want to be located far away or enclosed in their temporary coordinates, but seek instead to reach our experience, the present?

[…]

Is it necessary to know how to cross this perhaps tormented discretion in order to plumb the depths of Rafael Moneo's architecture, as a diagnosis and proposal for taking action in our times? Moneo's attempt, which can be perceived only by applying what has been written on other architects to him, too, can be located on ground on the other side of the street, from where we can take in Venturi and Gehry with only one glance.

The unknown, linguistic negativity[3] would be the condition that might enable architecture to realize

its own collective nature – outside of rhetoric, its own nature as public work – thus leaving aside the desire to proclaim itself a "work of art". It is Jacob's struggle to compress the time of architecture – to offer us all of it in a single instant of infinite duration, it would tell us of the end of Progress, of the end of time understood as a triumphal march of the calendar, of time in which the empty, uniform beat is nothing other than the rhythm that we are all counted in.
[…]
Erudite archeologists have dug in the fossilized point of my time: do not be embittered for us when you discover that we are contemporaries of the strata of disaster. I was part of the time when Sánchez Ferlosio wrote, Erice filmed, García Calvo spoke, Lopez García painted and Rafael Moneo built.
Know us all through them and be invidious of us, at least, for having made part of their time.

[1] The allusion, in this case, is the *L'ultimo paradosso* by Alberto Asor Rosa.
[2] Rafael Moneo, "A la conquista de lo irracional", in *Arquitectura*, 87, March 1966, p. 1.
[3] Which idiots call "eclecticism".

J. Quetglas, "The dance and the procession. The shape of time in the architecture of Rafael Moneo", in *Rafael Moneo 1990-1994*, El Croquis monograph no. 64, 1994, pp. 27-45 (translation by Antonella Bergamin).

Giovanni Leoni
Rafael Moneo: Architecture as Architecture

The contemporary world, wrote Moneo in his text *L'idea di durata e i materiali della costruzione* (1988, Italian translation in R. Moneo, *La solitudine degli edifici*) puts a great deal of pressure, both economic and cultural, on the architect to give abstract answers, and a building programme is always of necessity guided by an ideological mandate. But the building cannot be a simple expression of an idea, it must undergo a process of materialization. This process, as becomes clear in

what is perhaps the densest manifesto of architecture that it is difficult to encapsulate in theoretical formulations, or *The solitude of buildings* (Kenzo Tange Lecture, Harvard, 9 March 1985, partially translated in *Casabella*, n. 666, Apr. 1999, pp. 30-33), does not come about automatically because of construction, which can also be a simple transcription of design into reality. And there is no doubt that, so to speak, Moneo grasps one of the most evident characteristics of contemporary architecture, the one which more than all the others makes it unpopular to the common mentality – that is to say, the incapacity to seem real, to leave the realm of representation. This comes about, again according to Moneo, because "today many architects invent methods or they master techniques of design with no relation to the reality of building", not understanding that design must be only an instrument of control, while architecture is "a complex reality that implies different presences" which "are reflected in that multiple mirror that is the building".
The goal indicated by Moneo is, to think about it, paradoxical. What he requires of architecture, which is a technical practice subject to collective procedures and which would thus be paralyzed without communication and without representation, is to go beyond representation. But here it is a question of a useful paradox, which in fact does not simply consist of knowing and accepting, perhaps reluctantly as happens for the most part with contemporary architects, that the building will have an uncertain life of its own once constructed, but rather of bringing back inside the horizon of the project the future life of the building that cannot be controlled from the project. The final task of the architect is to lead the building to the threshold of this life and to prepare it for that life; it is to create the conditions for an act of detachment from architecture, which would deliver it to the world not as form, which would be destroyed by the world since it is fragile, but as a thing among things. Obviously re-comprehension in the project of a life of the building that cannot be designed or controlled is not obtained by trusting in an improbable immediacy and spontaneity. On the contrary, it can be reached only

through constructional discipline that progressively intuits, and then lets prevail, an inner logic of the architectural object, finally taking the domain from the inventor. Thus there is no need for less project, but more project, a project that is so rigorous and controlled in every aspect and detail as to be able to be led to its completion, and as a consequence, to its disappearance as such; a project that is willing to fade into becoming the thing of architecture. "Architecture implies a distance between ourselves and the work in such a way that in the end, the work stands alone, capable of holding itself up once it has acquired its own physical consistency. Our pleasure stands in the experience of this distance, when we see our thought given substance in a reality that no longer belongs to us."

One of the most interesting themes with regard to the greater control of the project, according to Moneo, necessary in order to transform the building into a real object is the re-thinking that he suggests for the relationships between design and building practice, indicating the need to recover lost coherence between the ideational and constructional design, which in current project practice have arrived at being languages that are for the most part completely foreign. In past periods, writes Moneo, "before being designed, a design implied certain constructional conventions. Only recently, perhaps with some Illuminist architects, has the connection between graphic expression and building knowledge begun to dissolve." Evidently, the coherence to be recovered can only be entrusted to the school and to the institution of a closer bond between designer and builder, a bond based not only on relationships of an economic nature, but also on the sharing of a body of architectural knowledge. "Architects must accept techniques and use building systems to start up the process of formal invention that is then concluded with architecture… traditionally, being an architect implied the necessity of being a builder, which meant explaining to others how to build. Knowledge of building techniques (if not mastery in them) was always implicit in the idea of producing architecture."

The building is thus given over to the world as a

thing, and it is perhaps the only negative act allowed to the architectural discipline, not the negation of form, not the negation of construction, not the negation of presence – or the principal attempts at the negation of architecture tried in the twentieth century: decomposition, deconstruction, minimalism – but delivering the building to reality, a negative act for the inventor's individuality, but definitely productive for the existence of the building.

G. Leoni, *Rafael Moneo: architettura come architettura*, in Area monograph no. 67, 2003, pp. 6-31.

Daniele Vitale
Introduction to Rafael Moneo's The Solitude of Buildings and Other Writings

The time given to humans goes by rapidly and unpredictably. Their memory is fragile. That is why they tend to identify events with things. For this reason they aspire to building landscapes that have stability. Only by imagining correspondences with things can the memory conquer its mutability and define a picture, only in this way can it find a way to perpetuate itself and acquire collective breathing space.

Thus the destiny of architecture is singular: since it was born to correspond to concrete needs, but places itself as a factor of recognition and identity, it immediately goes beyond and transcends them. This explains the special quality of its rapport with time. The city and the landscape are slowly formed in time, and feed upon it; but they also represent a way of stopping time, of holding it back, of enclosing it in the outlines of a form. In the body and in the form, they reveal their inner depth, almost as if there were a mysterious resonance of ages and generations inside them. Architecture takes part in this resonance.

Few contemporary architects have known this depth and these rites like Rafael Moneo. Few understand how much actuality is entangled in the experience of history. In considering the question of the Mosque in Cordova, he talks about the life of buildings, and he speaks of them as having life that is distinct from that of human life. In his words, there is an echo of John Ruskin and his "Lamp of Memory"[1]. Every building, by force of circumstances and by implicit destiny, is the object of transformations, of adaptations, of reconstructions. But if it is based on formal principles that are sufficiently clear, if it is permeated by an ideal structure, then it will be capable of conserving its own identity and continuing to be recognized, changing according to the thread of an inner continuity.

Architecture is in fact this essential scheme, this totality of kinds of logic and of forms that condition change and make continuity possible. Every building, and more than buildings, every city, lives in this tension between an underlying scheme and the changes wrought, between a system that gives order and the juxtaposition of events.

The writings collected here are diverse – in inspiration and in theme, by period and occasion – but they are constructed around a central nucleus of ideas enriched by work and by the years: and in this way, following one after another, they gradually unwind the thread of a discourse. It is not a book of theory, because perhaps a theory in present conditions is not given: but a reflection that draws upon history and that is nourished by a living interest for the world, conducted by an architect-intellectual committed to his profession, who looks at buildings with the eye of someone who must once again confront problems they have already given an answer to. The writings draw their strength and intensity from this *inner* placement with ties to making architecture: so that observation and meditation remain intensely interrelated there; so that the intellectual construction is placed in constant tension with the world of objects and things. Once upon a time the work of art and the literary work, equal to the work of architecture, were fed and permeated by a doctrinal *corpus* that aspired to completeness based on closed systems. However, in the modern condition, criticism, with its abilities of analysis and comparison, conquers new space and agrees in constructing thought, to the point of assuming a role in the work and becoming the midwife of choices.

In Moneo's writings, in their superimposing contemplation and *self-contemplation*, and in their constantly referring to works and projects, I see a reflection of this condition of modern art and literature, and at the same time, a return to the specific tradition of architects, for whom the logic of discourse and the logic of forms are placed in opposition to one another, in a necessary, unresolved dialectic.

However, his is always intelligence of architecture for *figures*. Only by passing through the shapes in which things are made real is it possible to approach architecture. It is not reduced to what is visible and does not coincide with an exterior game of appearances: shapes are a means *to go beyond*, to discover the profound reality and inner nature of things. Leonardo believed in the mental value of images, as if they belonged more to the sphere of consciousness than to the domain of the eye[2]. And his was not only an idea of drawing and painting, but also of man's relationship with the world.

But all of this presupposes an idea of the substantial *alterity* of architecture with respect to the life of human beings: an alternative idea to one that, with modernity, thought of linearly connecting the choices involved in architecture to those of social organization and progress. The *solitude of buildings*, says the title: because, like all things man constructs, once buildings are finished, they are separated from the feelings and passions that accompanied them up to that point, from circumstances, from intentions, from models. At first, they are born on the basis of a request and a need, in relation to a place and a society, within a system of tensions and conflicts: but those conflicts sublimate and are fixed in form. In the end, only the object, only the artifact remains. Thus they silently enter into a sort of «second nature», in a realm of things where all of a sudden they find a network of relationships, discovering contrasts and affinities, enemies and kinship.

However, a building also has an analytical character, and is composed of elements that were there before it was. The elements are to the building what words are to speech.

I do not see with my eyes: words
are my eyes. We live amidst names;
whatever does not have a name does not exist
yet...[3]

First of all, words are what we all inherit. They are the tools of recognition and intelligence in the world, a way of approaching things by denoting them. But words precede phrases, they come before speech and its possibilities. Words, too, are expressive, but with respect to speech, their expressiveness is more or less confined and relative. The same thing also happens in architecture. A stone, natural or treated, is little more than a found object or an available element: but a wall of stones changes the meaning of each one and magnifies its possibilities, elevating them to higher, more complex reality. Stone in itself is neither beautiful nor ugly. Beauty is composition of elements that are irrelevant when considered individually. Beauty always refers to the whole, to the construction. Moneo knows that one cannot speak without using words, and that words are given. He knows that only through them can one express himself or herself. He knows that every invention is born of known things. He knows the value of the disposition and composition of elements and the variety of routes that open up. But at the same time he knows the value and force of the image and its simplicity.

In his writings in the Durand's manual at the beginning of the nineteenth century[4], he considers what "composition" was for him, and what it often returns to be today, that is to say, a combinatory game, a clever method that can bring needs and programmes back to mechanisms of geometric control and formal elaboration. And he implicitly suggests a different route, where the elements of a building do not only obey the logic of disposition, but rather an ideal layout, where architecture, measuring itself up against circumstances, remains nonetheless capable of drawing on more profound experiences, reconnecting past and present, persisting in the manifestation of an essential, archaic undertaking, placing itself as creator of worlds.

Architecture does not construct with linear progression, but by discontinuous concatenations, through links and analogies after time as gone by, so much so that the latest work constructed can go back to the dawn of human experience and define itself transversally, though resonances and echoes. By nature, architecture is the osmosis of different temporalities, it lives of co-presences, includes the imminent and the remote, experience and actuality.

Thus it cannot be reduced to empirics and practical art: neither in its mere constructional and technological aspects, nor in the logic of a formal game or erudite make-up. In the composition of the elements, in the inlay of materials, in the wisdom of relationships, each time a symbolic code of the world is revealed. Even if the meanings cannot be separated from the code, and that is to say, from the mediation represented by systems and forms, architecture is by nature inhabited by the past and by myth: it reveals a gravity and a need that historical upheavals have not wiped out. Of course, tools, techniques and dimensions have changed, but what has not changed is the power of signs and their ability to be regenerated in relation to the profound and to the elementary.

[1] John Ruskin, *The Seven Lamps of Architecture*, 1st ed., Smith, Elder and Co., London, 1849. The work was then republished in *The Works of John Ruskin*, Ernest Thomas Cook and Alexander Wedderburn eds., 39 vols., G. Allen, London, 1903-1912, vol. VIII, pp. 3-272; Ruskin (1819-1900) tried to explain the role and meaning of architecture by using a system of "key words", first called "spirits" and then "lamps". The seven lamps are Sacrifice, Truth, Power, Beauty, Life, Memory and Obedience.

[2] "If you have contempt for Painting, which is only the imitator of all works evident in nature, you can be sure that you have contempt for a very subtle invention, which with philosophical and subtle speculation considers all of the qualities of forms... The deity that has the painter's science works in such a way that the mind of the painter is transformed into a likeness of the divine mind, since it operates freely in generating all kinds of animals, plants, fruits, villages, landscapes, ruins of mountains..." "And in effect whatever is in the universe by essence, frequency or imagination, he [the painter] has it first in his mind and then

in his hands" (cfr. Leonardo, *L'uomo e la natura*, ed. Mario De Micheli, Feltrinelli, Milan, 1991, p. 150, 152).

[3] Octavio Paz, *Pasado en claro*, Fondo de Cultura Económica, México, 1975. Republished in *Obras completas*, vol. 12, Fondo de Cultura, México, 2004. Paz (1914-1998) is an extraordinary Mexican poet and essayist.

[4] The second chapter of Moneo's book, *The Solitude of Buildings*, is entitled "Jean-Louis-Nicolas Durand's Teaching and the Elements of Composition". Durand (1760-1834), student of Boullée and professor of Composition from 1790 to 1835 at the École Polytechnique in Paris, was the author of theoretical texts and manuals that were widely circulated.

The main one was the *Précis des leçons d'architecture données à l'École Polytechnique*, 2 vols., 3 parts, chez l'auteur, à l'École Polytecnique, Paris, 1802-1805; 2nd ed. 1809; other eds. 1817-1819.

D. Vitale, Introduction to R. Moneo, *La solitudine degli edifici e altri scritti*, A. Casiraghi and D. Vitale eds. (collection of essays by Rafael Moneo published in 2 volumes, Umberto Allemandi & C., Turin-London; vol. I, *Questioni intorno all'architettura*, 1999; vol. II, *Sugli architetti e il loro lavoro*, 2004; translations by Andrea Casiraghi and Daniele Vitale).

Bibliography

R. Moneo, *Contro la indiferencia como forma*, Ediciones ARQ, Santiago, Chile 1995.

R. Moneo, *La solitudine degli edifici e altri scritti. Questioni intorno all'architettura* (Andrea Casiraghi, Daniele Vitale, eds.), Umberto Allemandi, Turin-London 1999.

R. Moneo, *Inquietudine teorica e strategia progettuale nell'opera di otto architetti contemporanei*, Mondadori Electa, Milan 2005.

R. Moneo, *Frank Lloyd Wright: Memorial Masieri, Venecia*, Editorial Rueda, S.L., Madrid 2005 (with the collaboration of Carmen Díez Medina and Valerio Canals Revilla).

Obras de Rafael Moneo, Hogar y Arquitectura monograph no. 76, 1968.

La obra arquitectónica de Rafael Moneo 1962-1974, Nueva Forma, 1975.

Josë Rafael Moneo, Boden, 1976.

Rafael Moneo, in *El Croquis*, monograph no. 20, 1985.

Rafael Moneo, in *a+u*, monograph no. 227, 1989.

Rafael Moneo. 1986-1992, A&V Monografías de Arquitectura y Vivienda, monograph no. 36, July-August 1992.

Rafael Moneo. Byggnsader Ochprojekt. 1973-1993, exhibit catalogue, Stockholm 1993-1994.

Rafael Moneo 1990-1994, in *El Croquis*, monograph no. 64, 1994.

E. Pinna, *Gli occhi della civetta. Impronte/Tracks*, interview, Electa, Milan, 1999.

Rafael Moneo. 1995-2000, in *El Croquis*, monograph no. 98, 2000.

Rafael Moneo, in *Area*, monograph no. 67, 2003.

Rafael Moneo. Obras recientes, in *Arkinka*, monograph no. 94, 2003.

F. Dal Co, "La Cattedrale di Nostra Signora Degli Angeli", interview in *Casabella*, 712, 2003.

Rafael Moneo. 1967-2004. Antología de urgencia / Imperative anthology, in *El Croquis*, 2004.

Rafael Moneo. Museoak Museos, Auditoriak Auditorios, Liburutegiak Bibliotecas, exhibit catalogue, Kubo-Artearen Kutxgunea, 2005.

El edificio del banco de España, exhibit catalogue, Madrid, 2006.

T. Vecci and A. Tartaglia, *Saper credere in architettura. Venti domande a Rafael Moneo*, interview, CLEAN edizioni, no. 32, 2007.